Bird

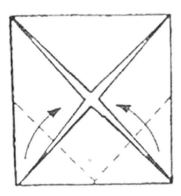

1

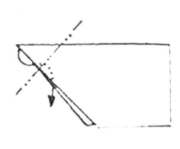

2

2

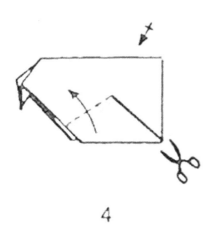

4

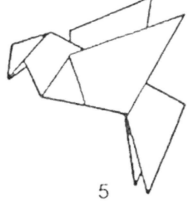

5

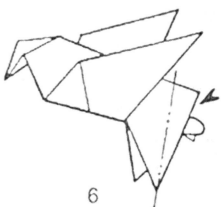

6

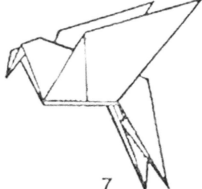

7

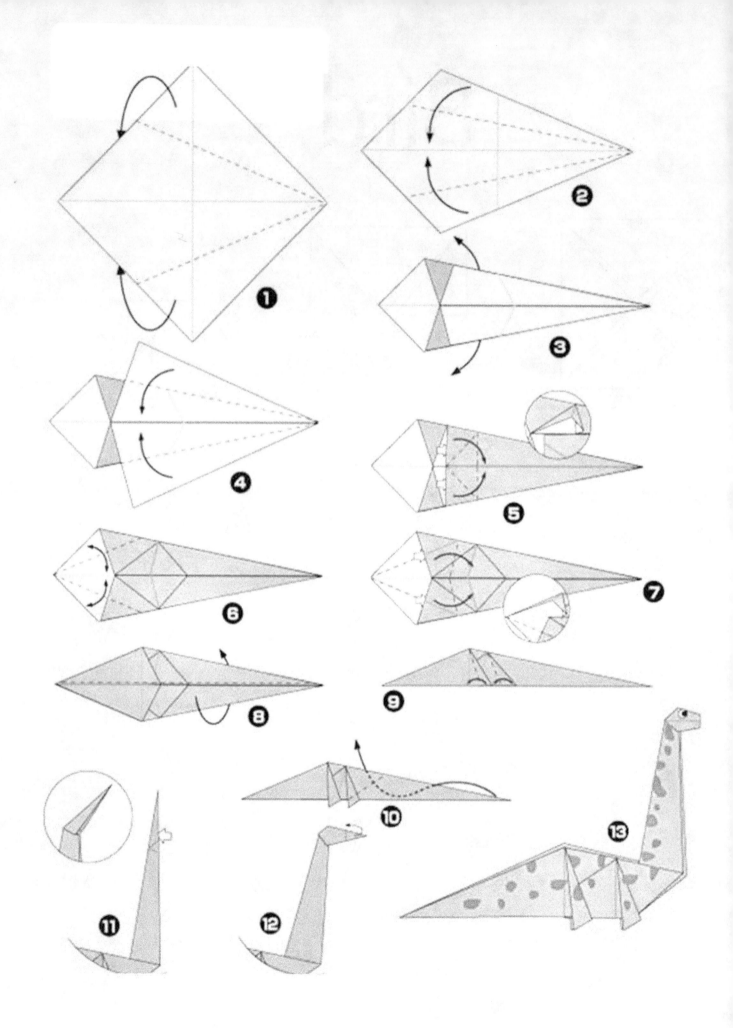

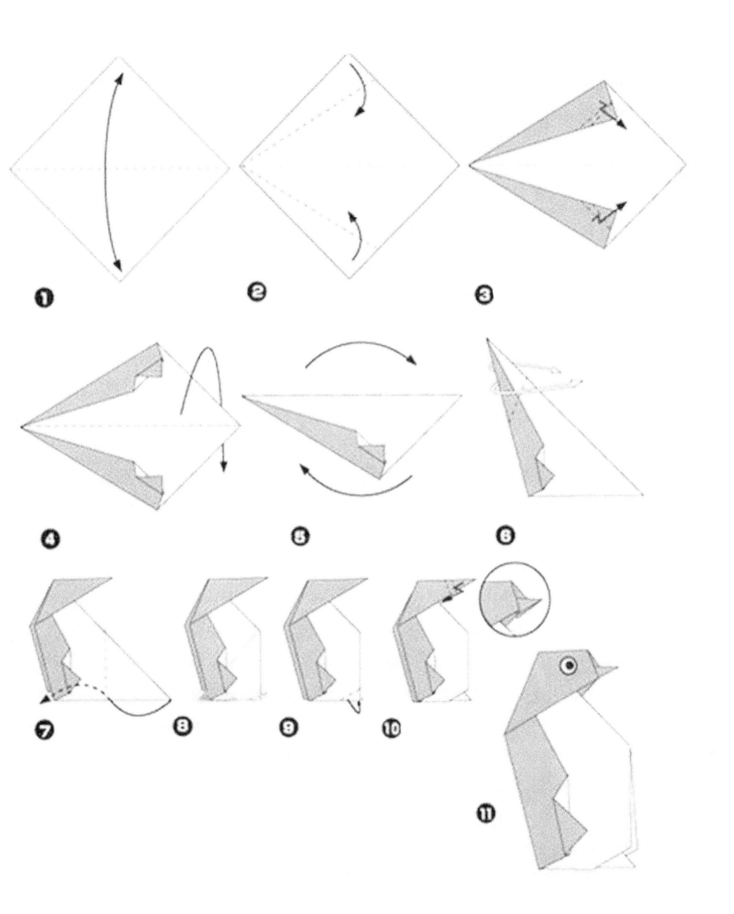

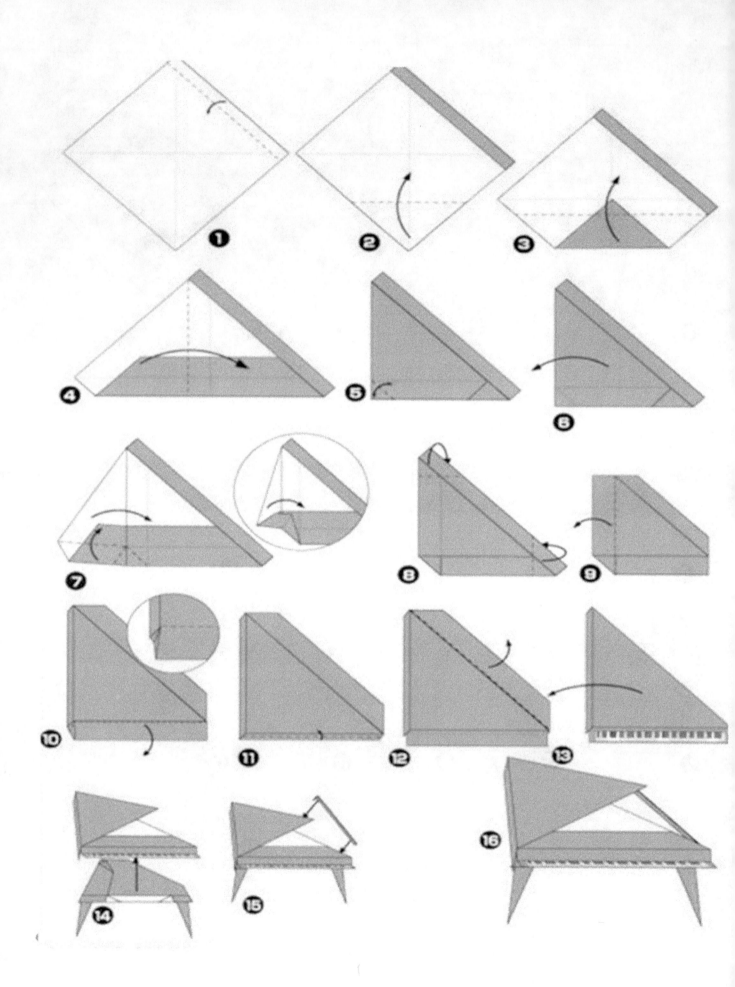

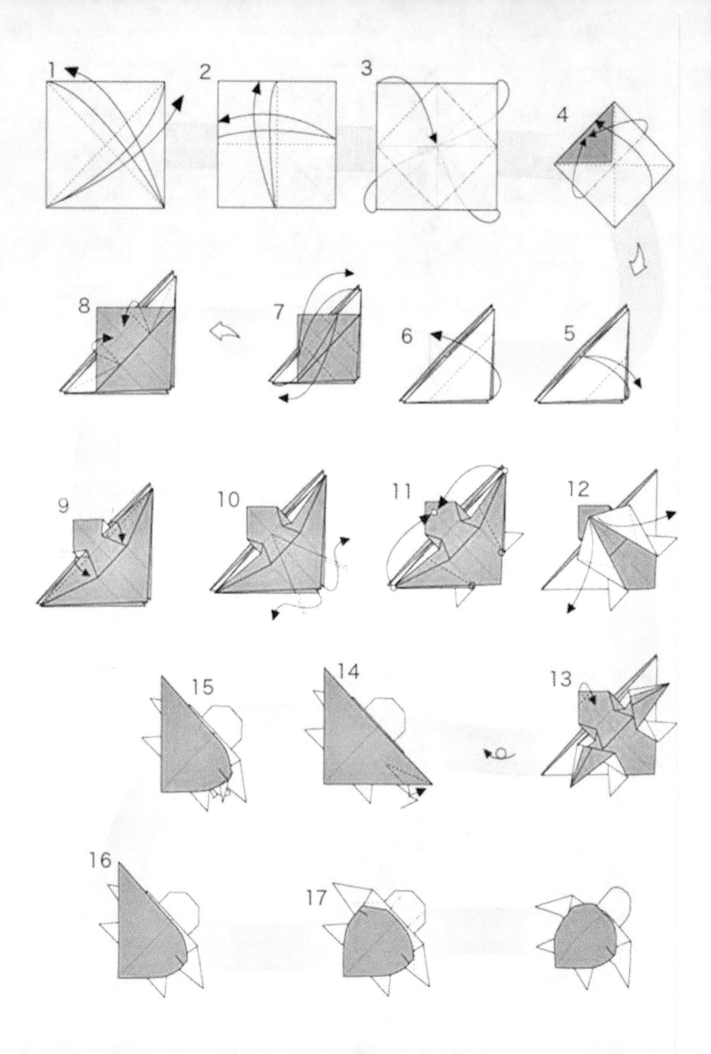

Boat (traditional)

Diagrammed by: František Grebeníček (1999)
www.origami.cz

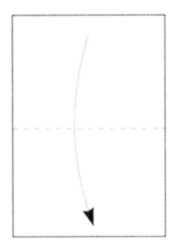

(1) Start from a rectangle (e.g. A4). Fold in half.

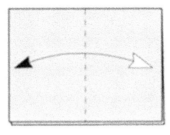

(2) Fold in half and unfold.

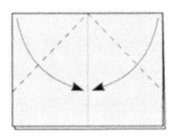

(3) Fold to the center.

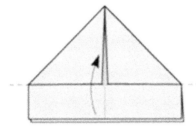

(4) Fold the overlapping strip upwards.

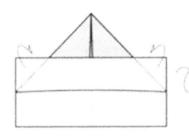

(5) Fold corners backwards. Turn over.

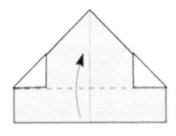

(6) Fold strip upwards.

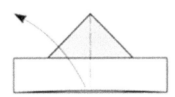

(7) Open.

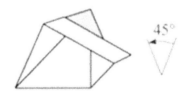

(8) Opening in progress.

(9) Fold triangle upwards. Repeat behind.

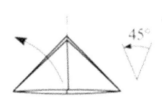

(10) Open (like in the steps 7 and 8).

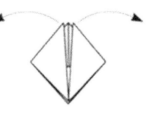

(11) Take upper corners and stretch out.

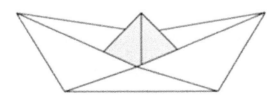

(12) Finished boat.

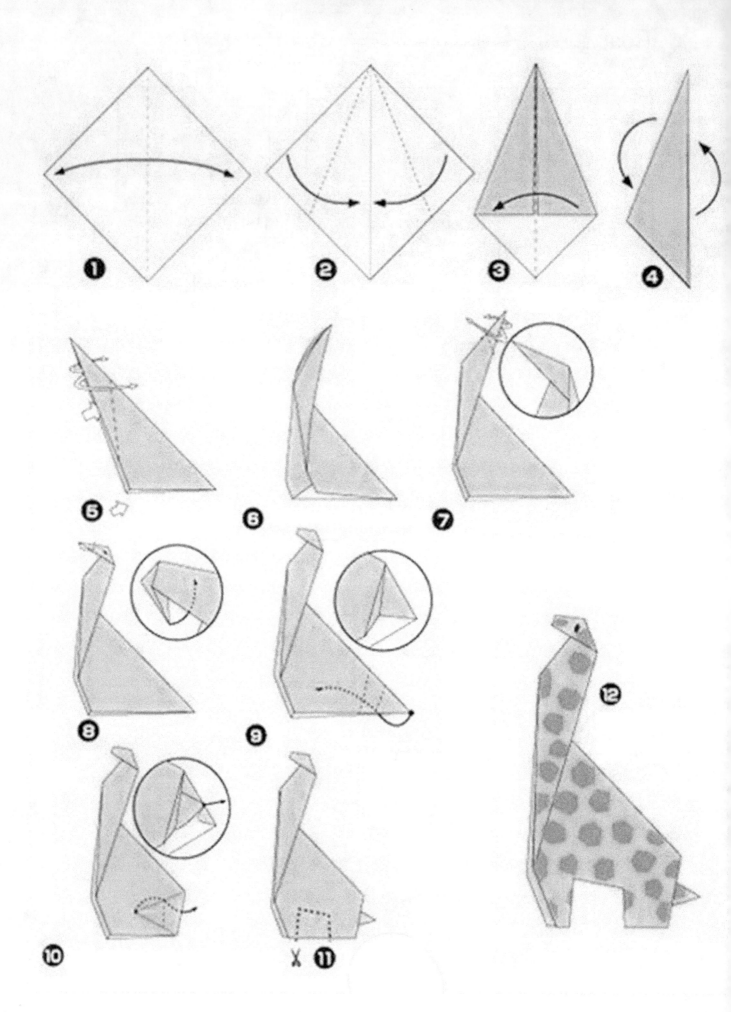

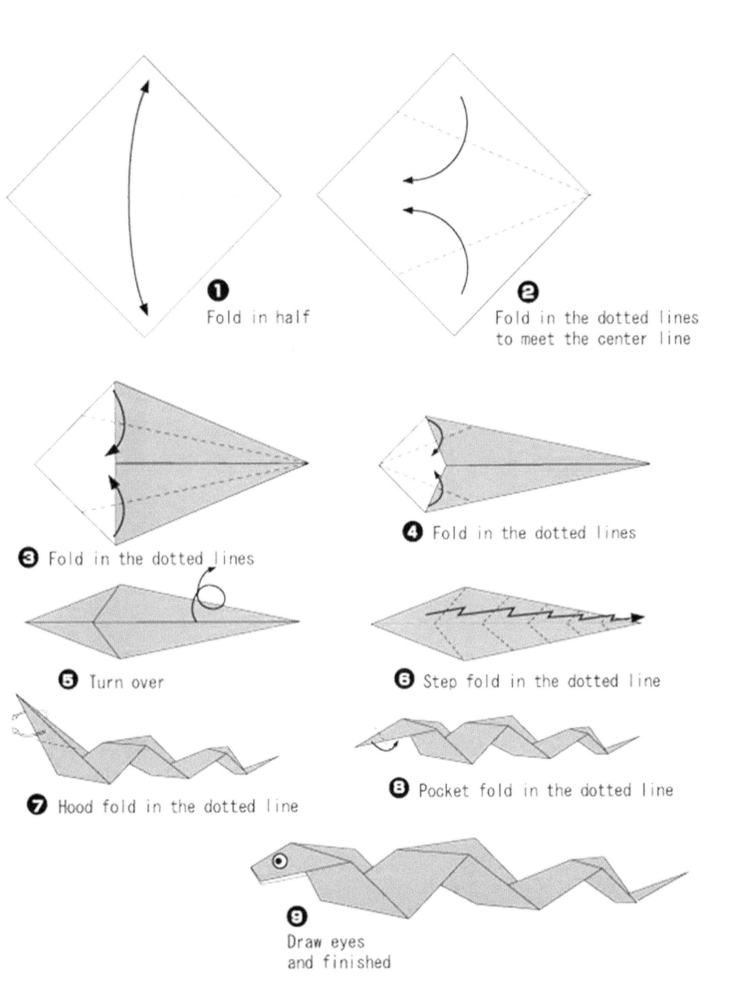

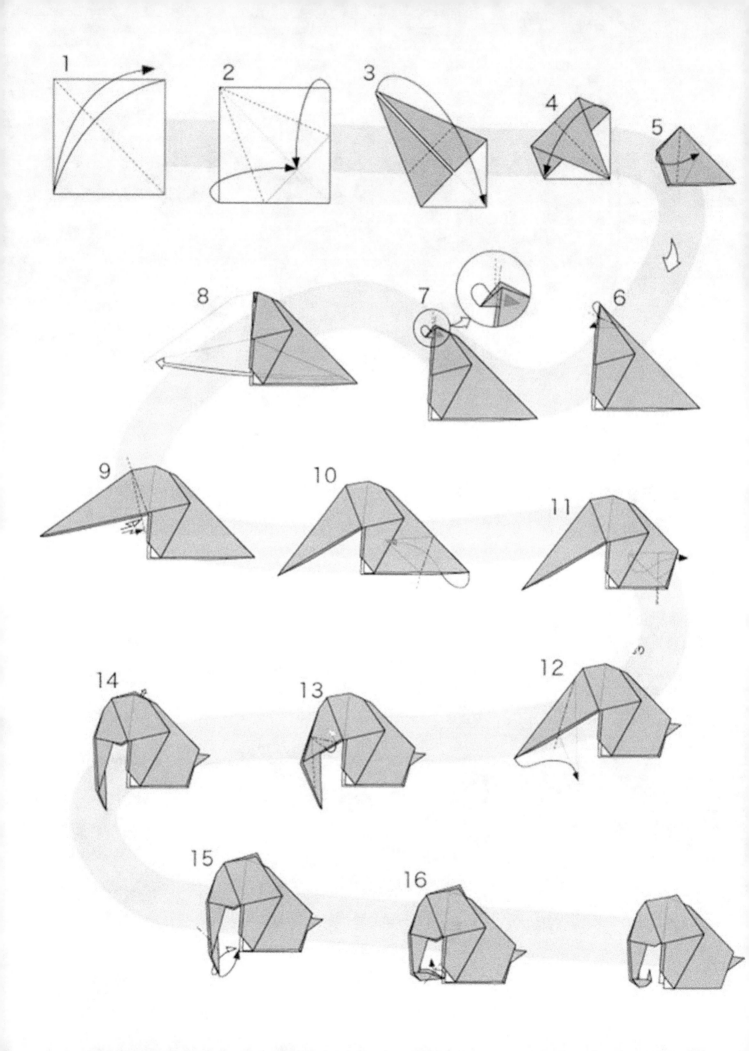

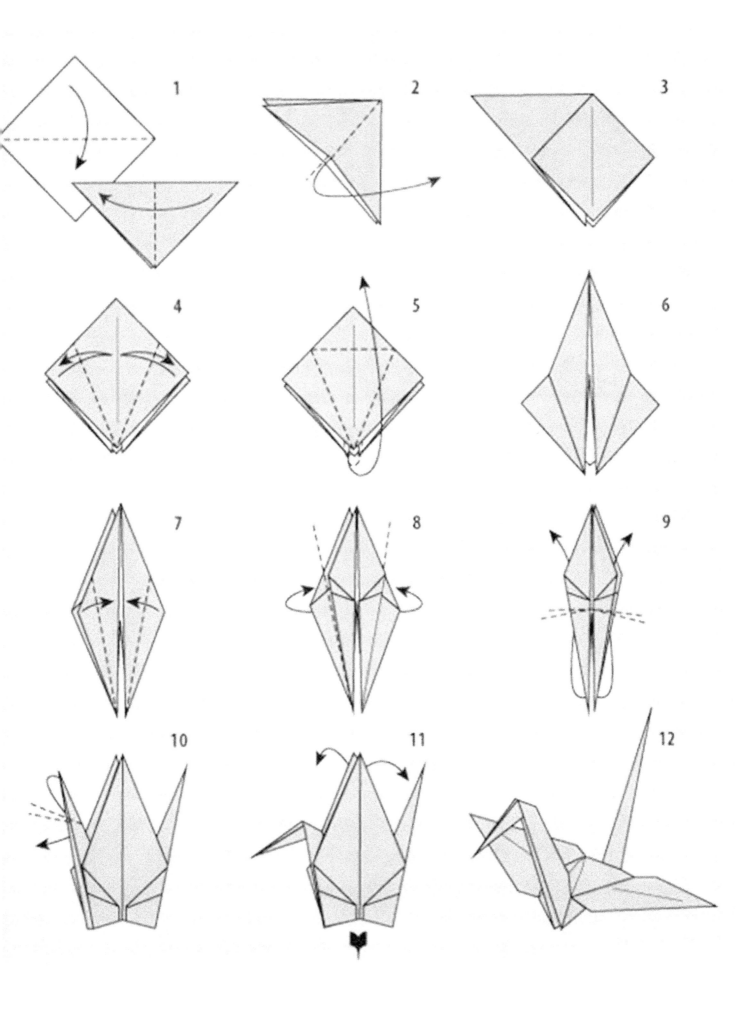

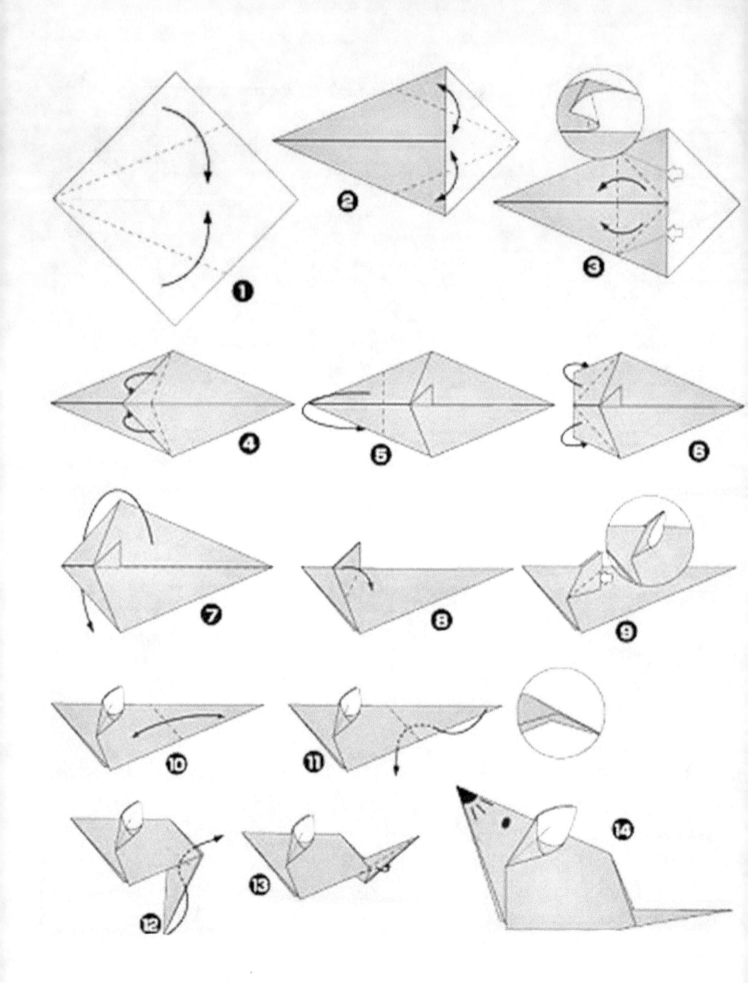

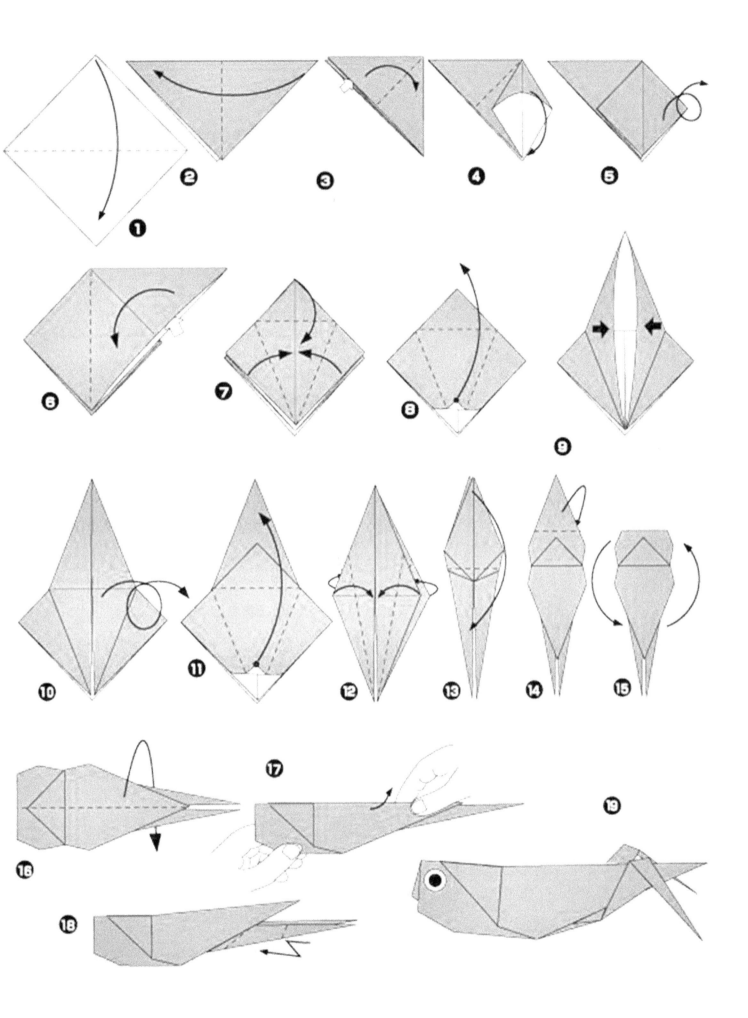

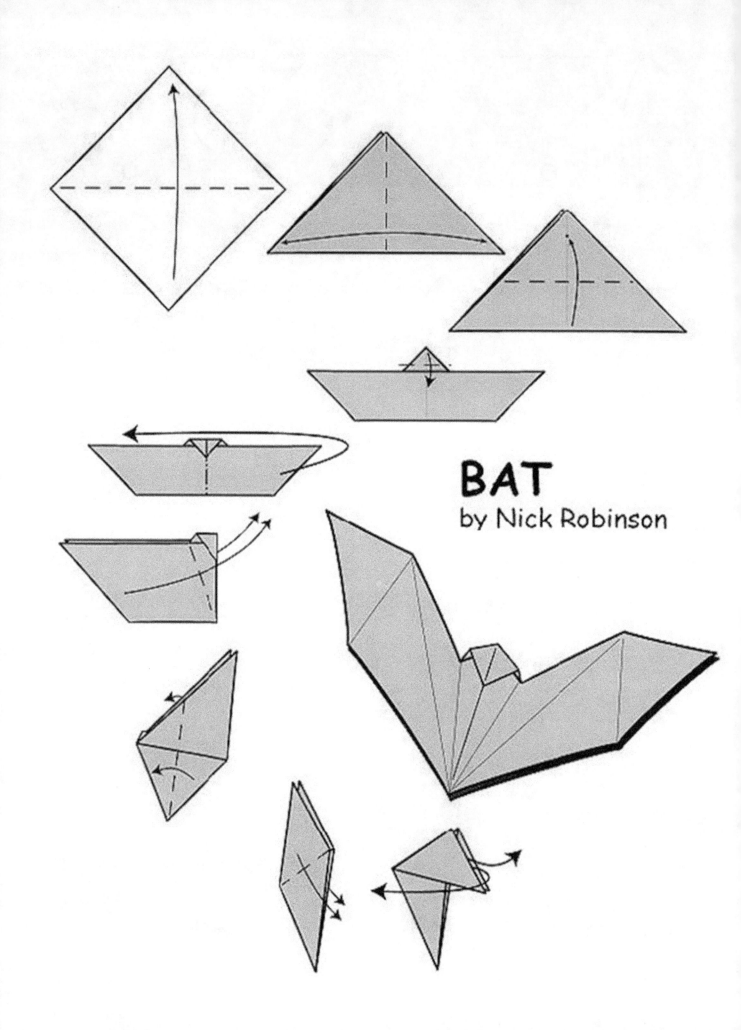

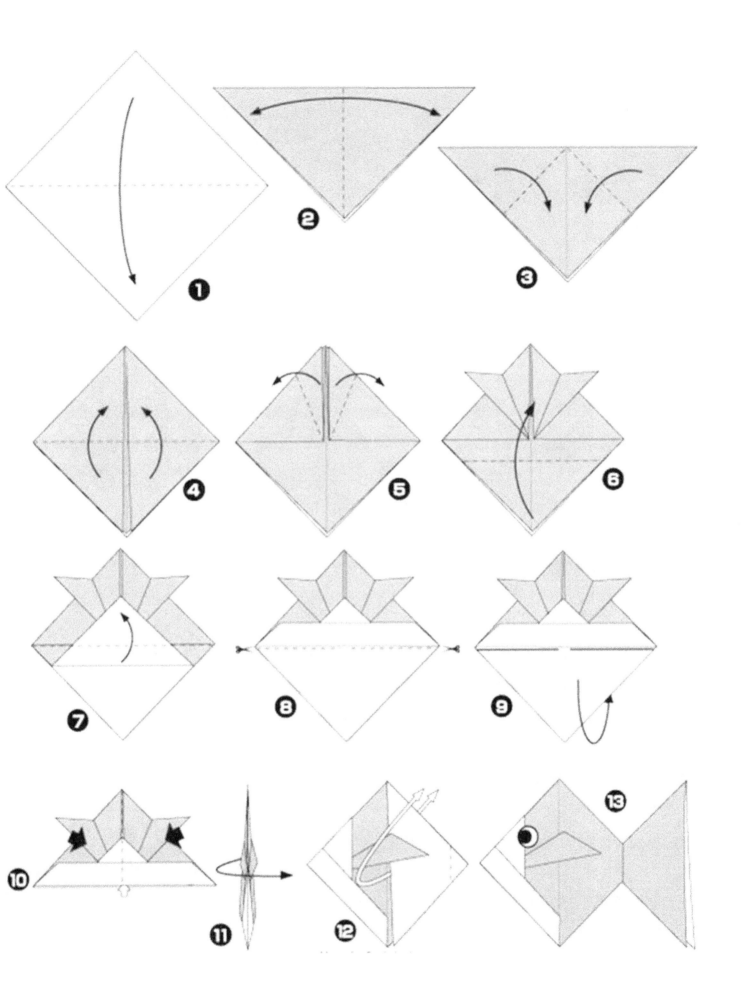

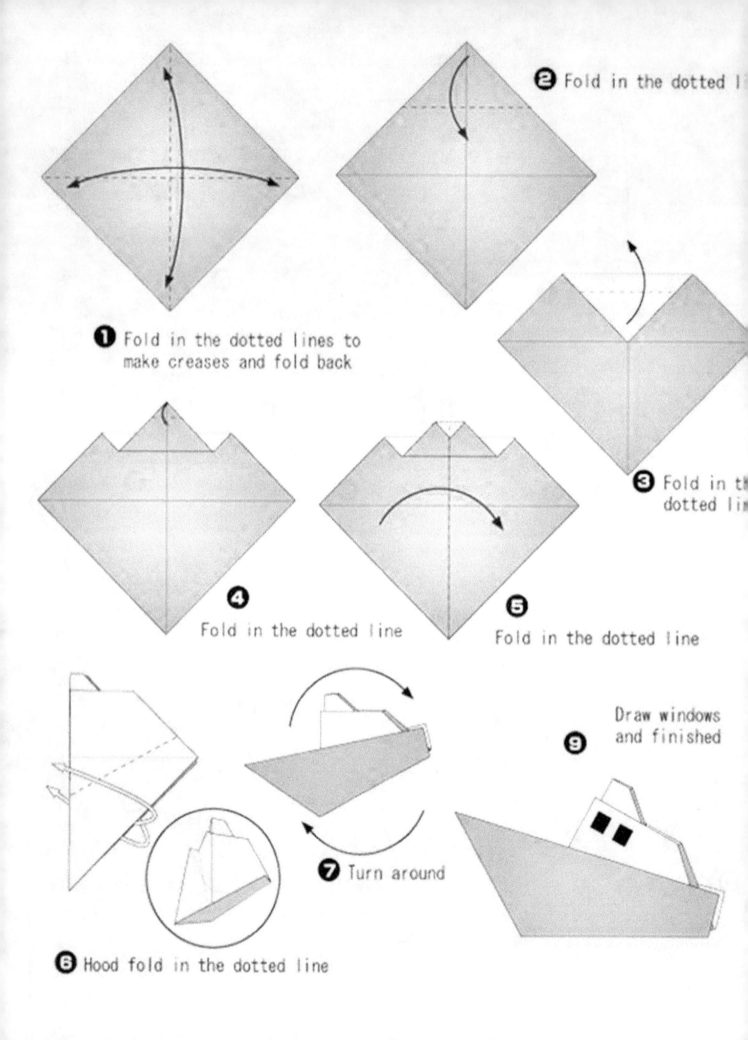

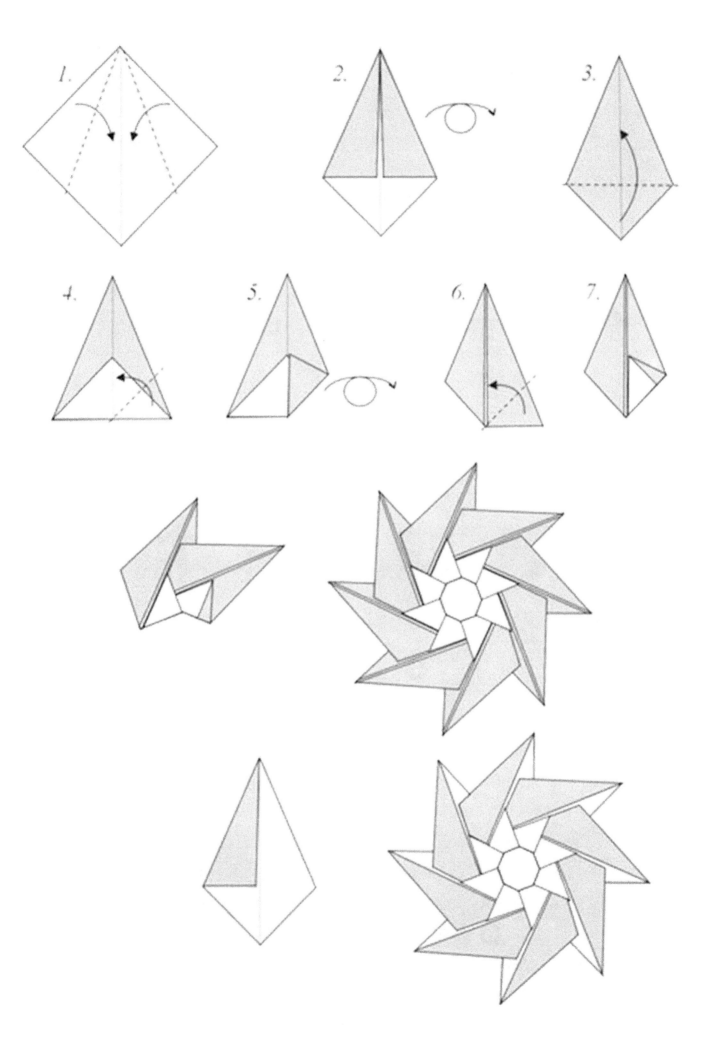

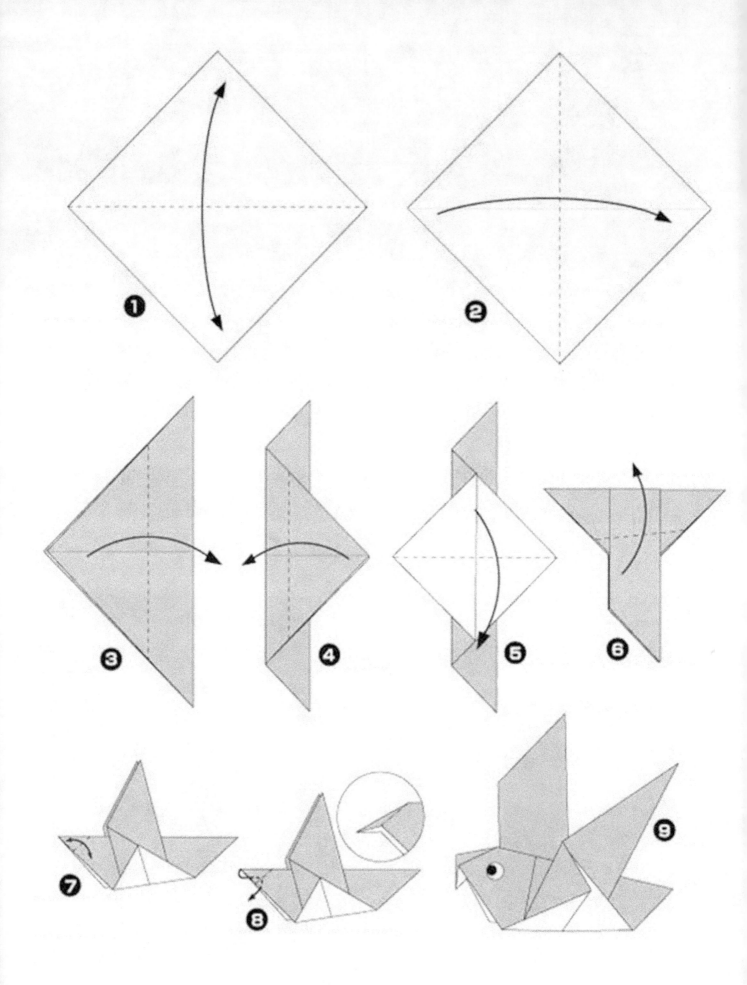

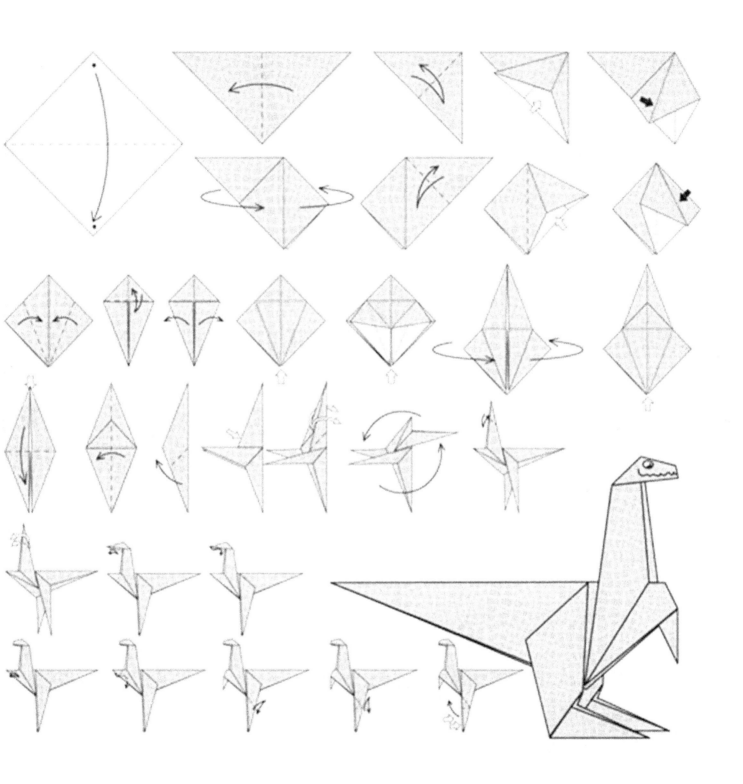

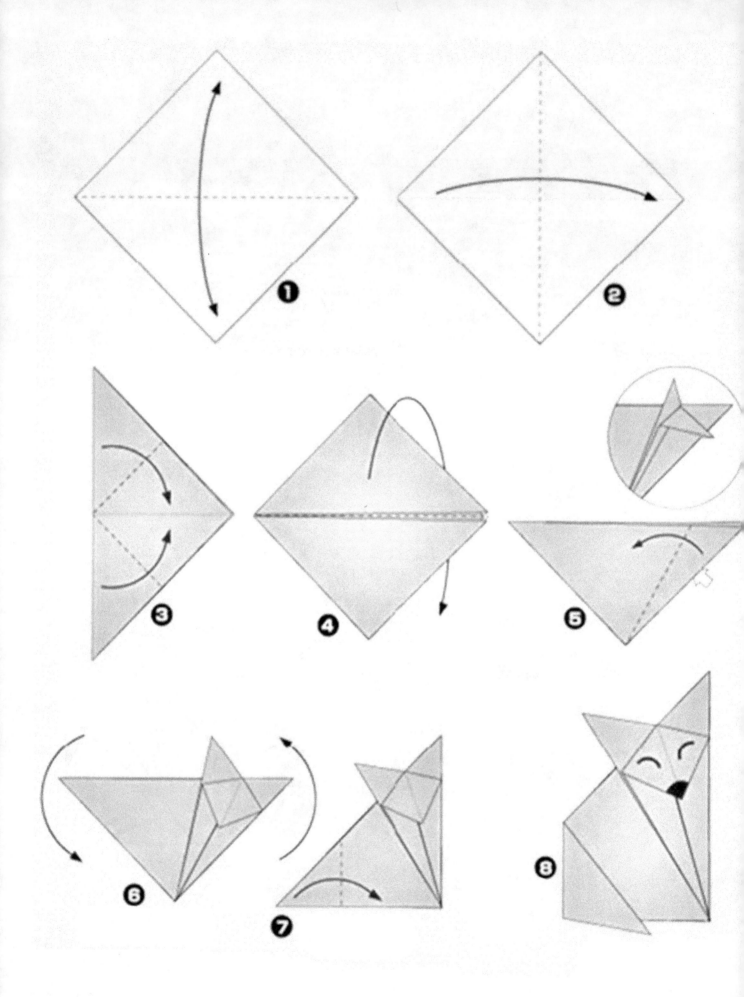

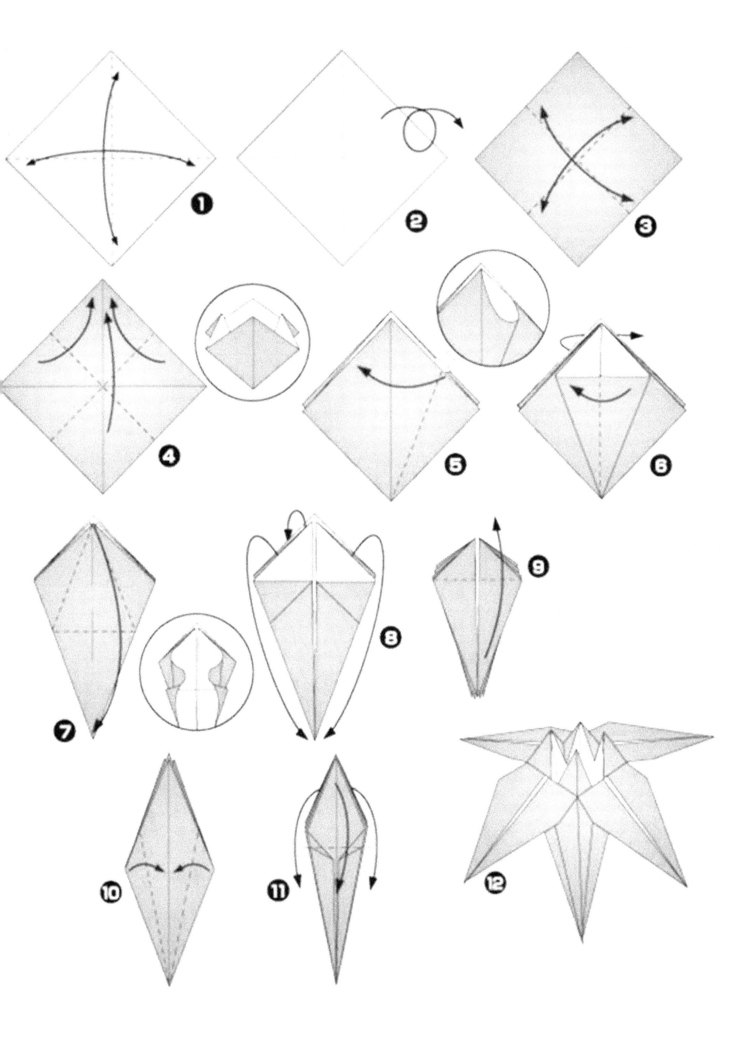

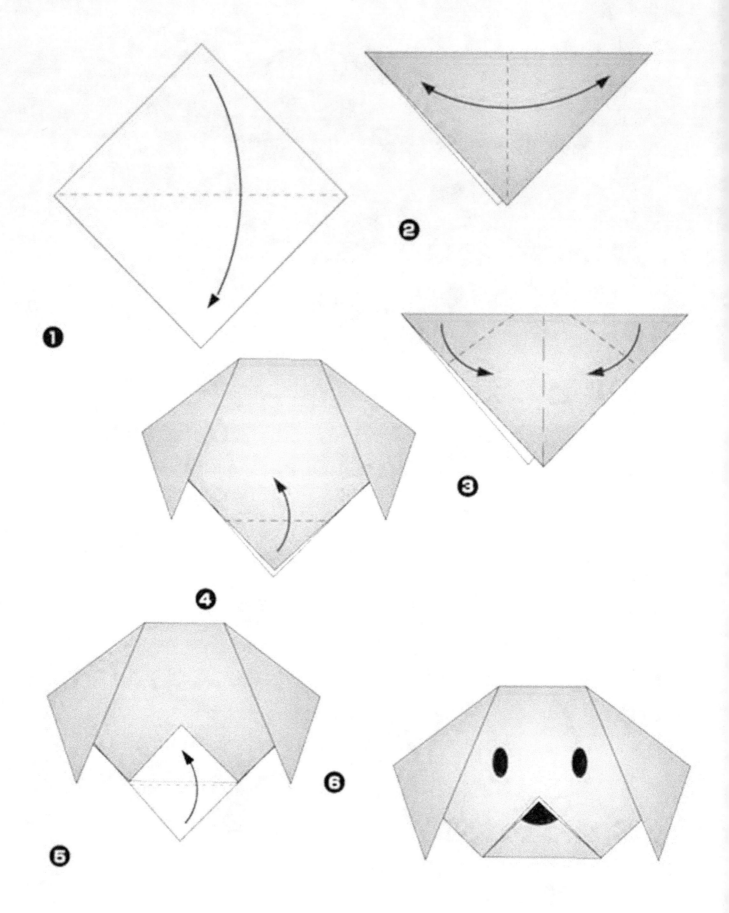

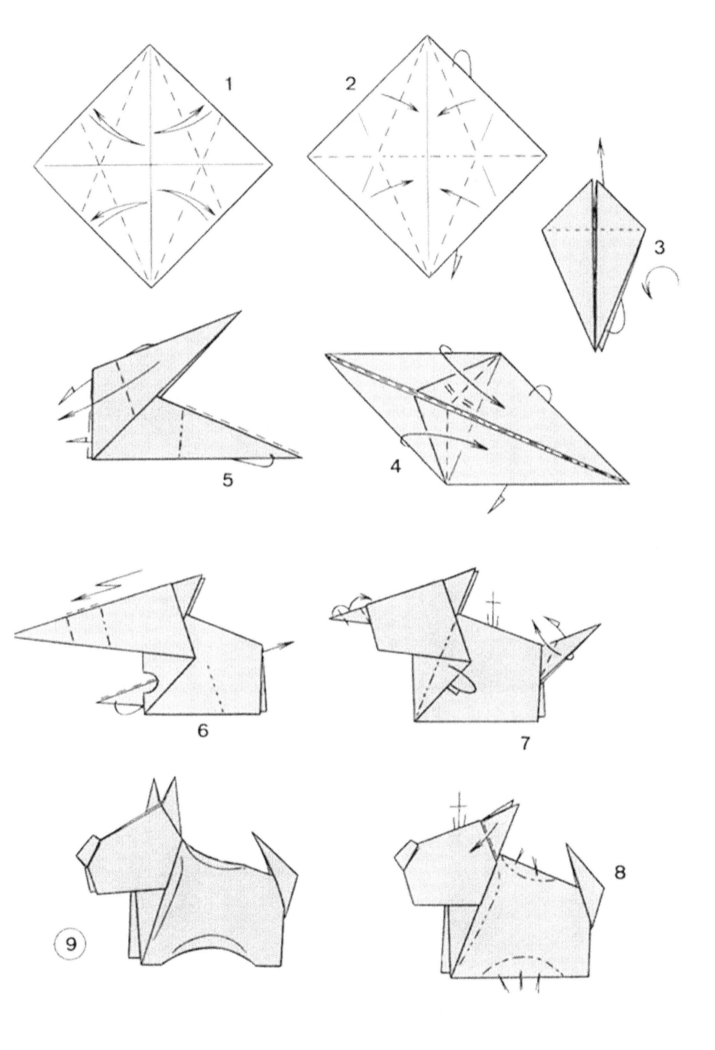

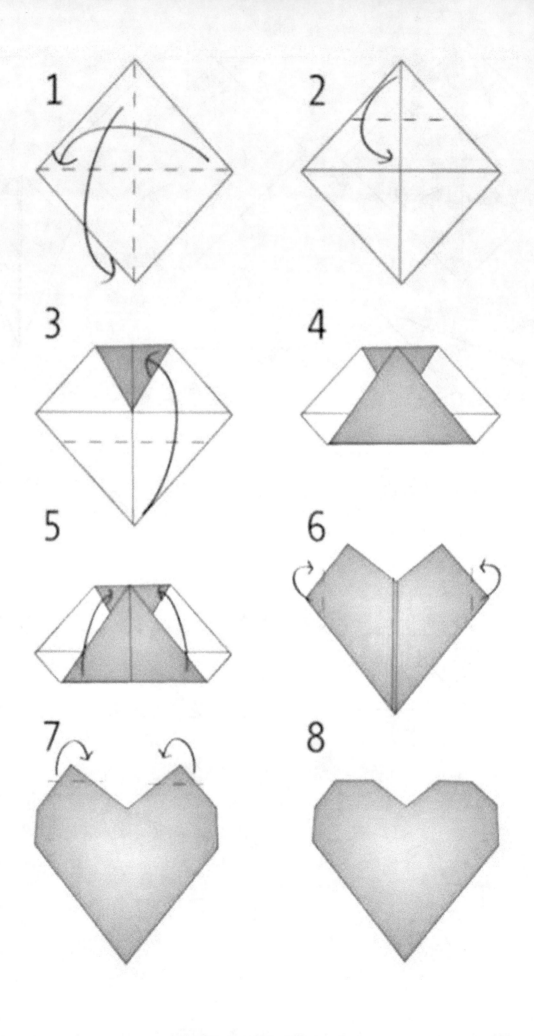

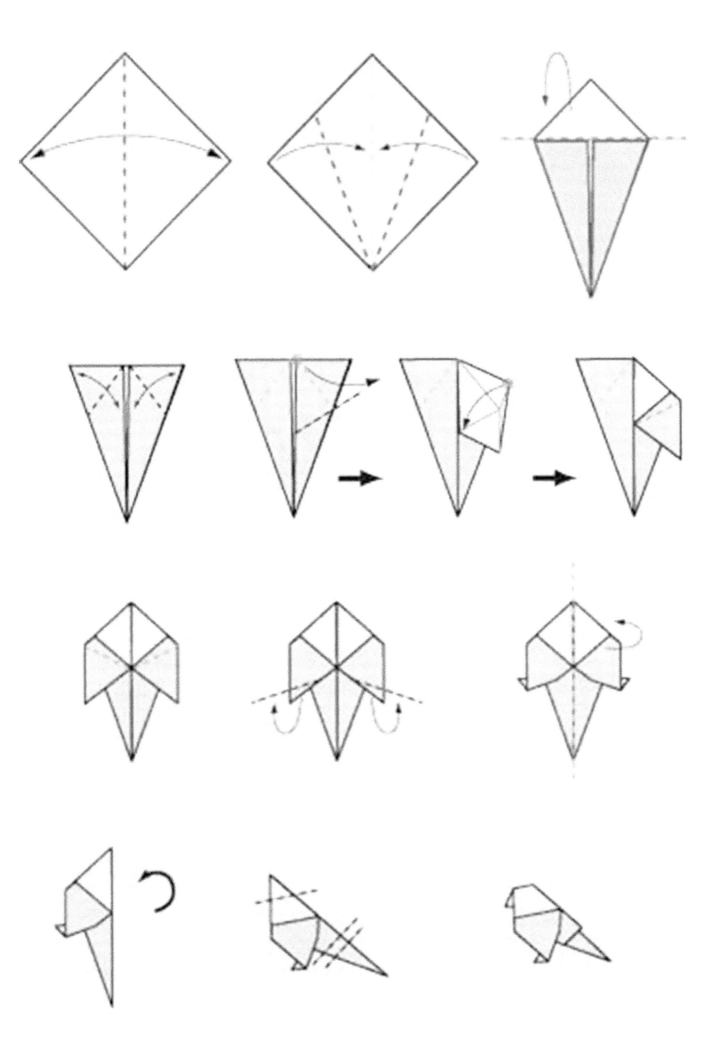

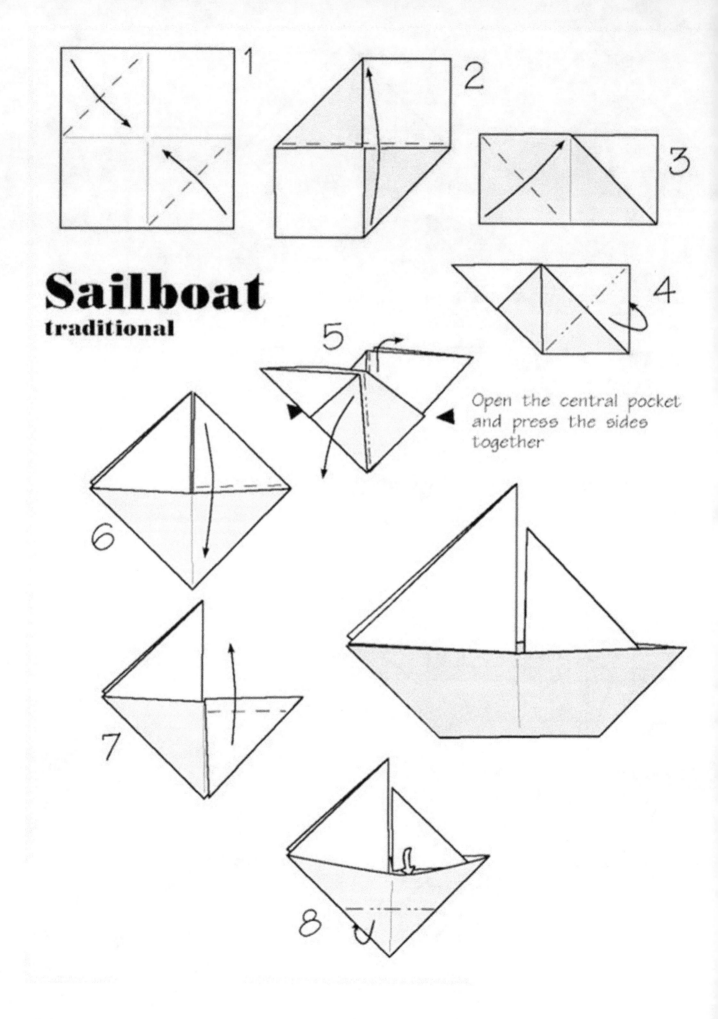

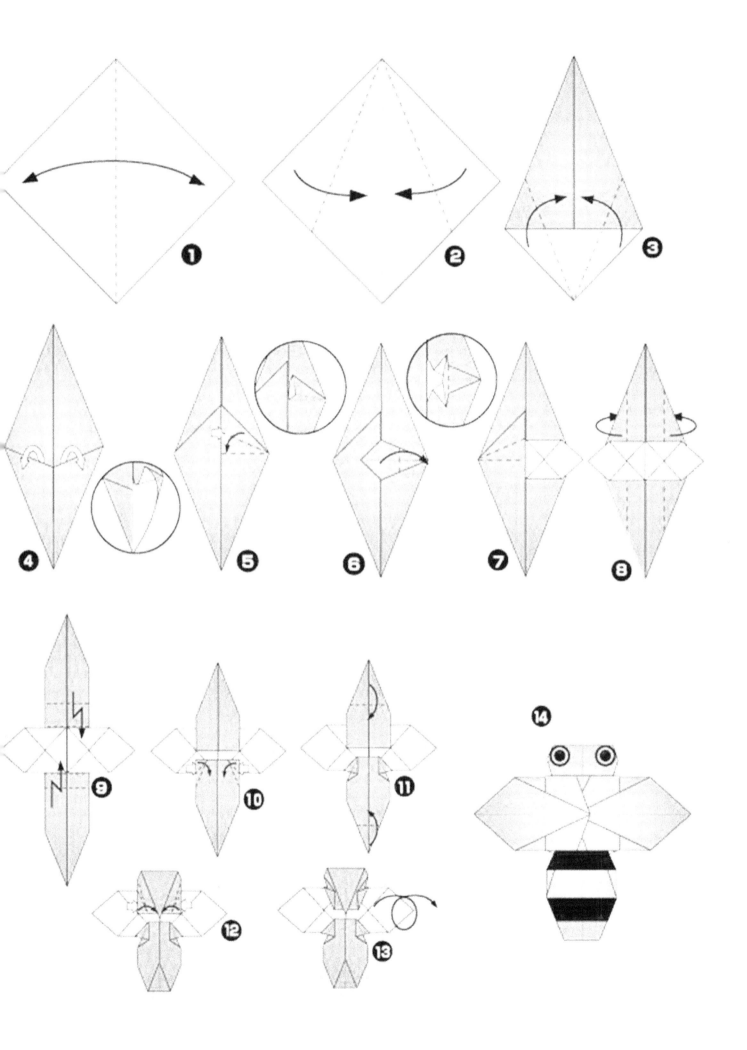

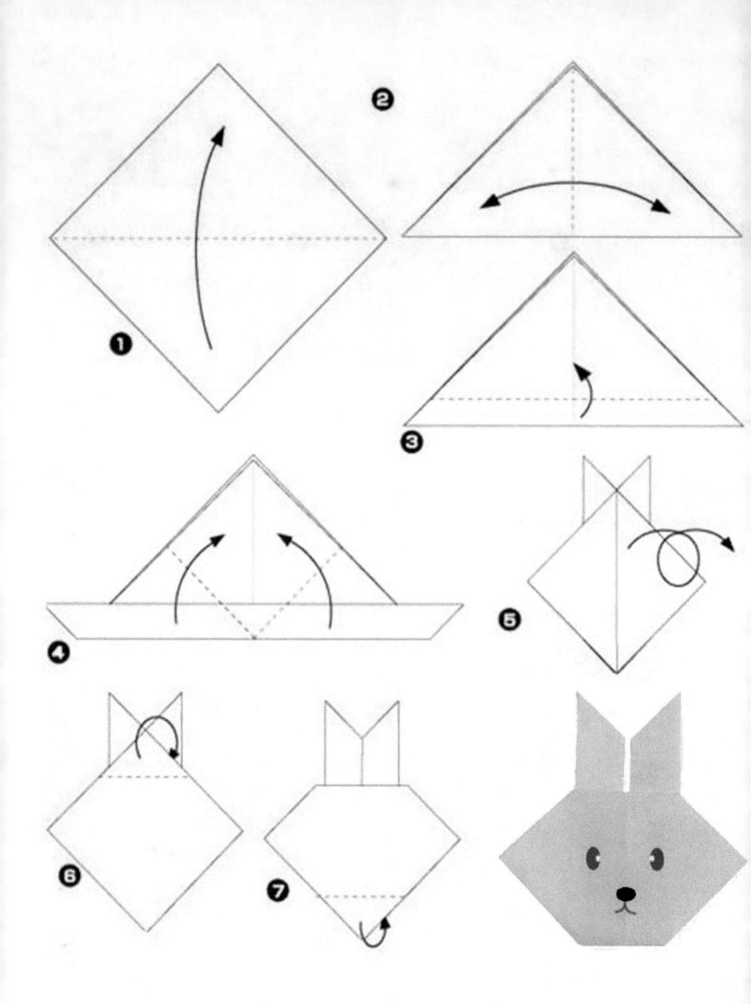

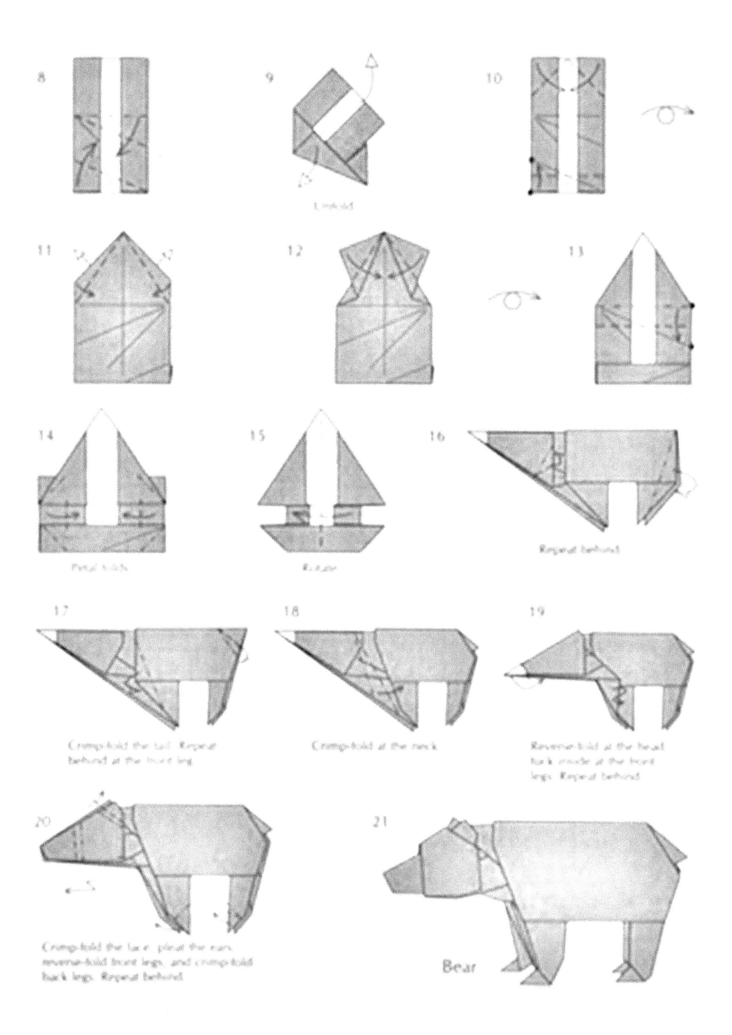

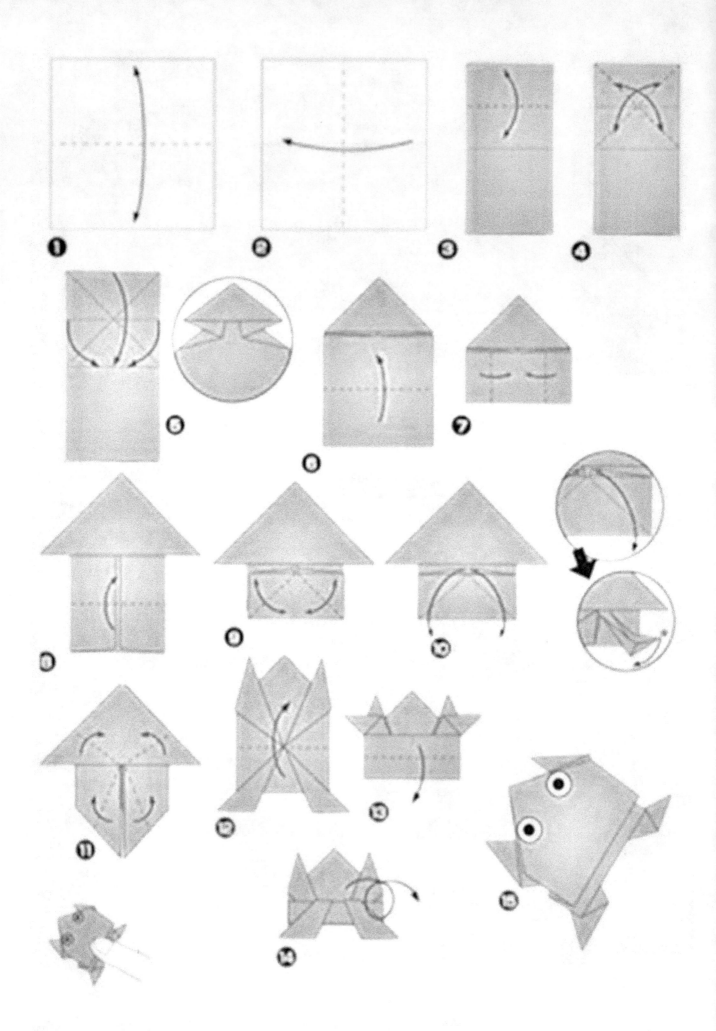

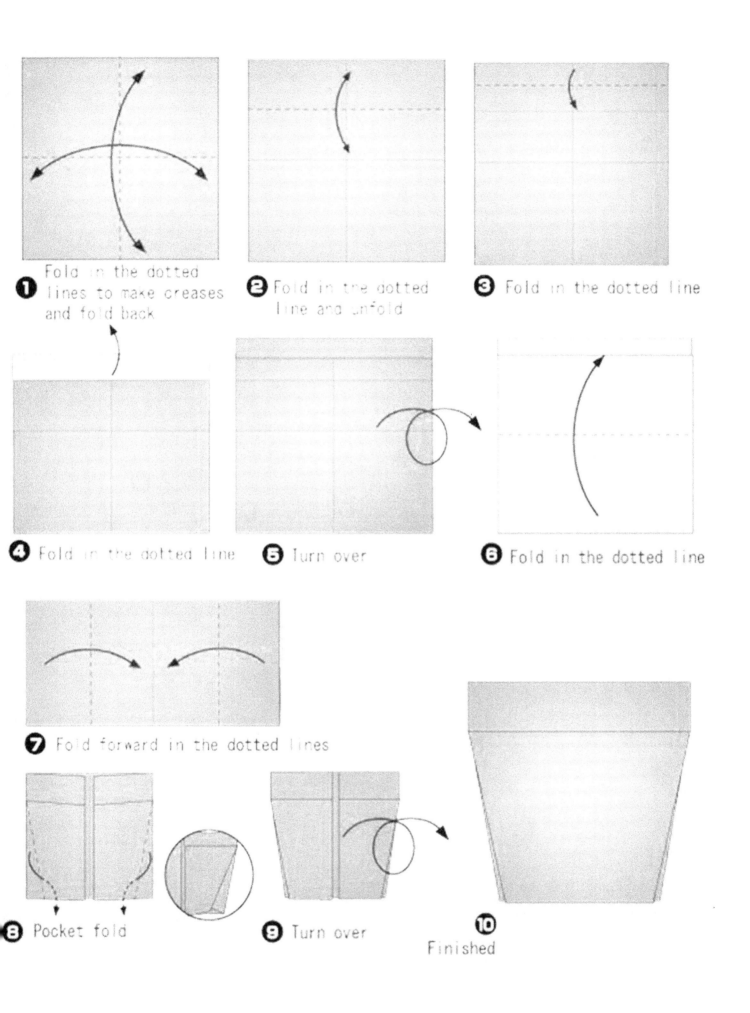

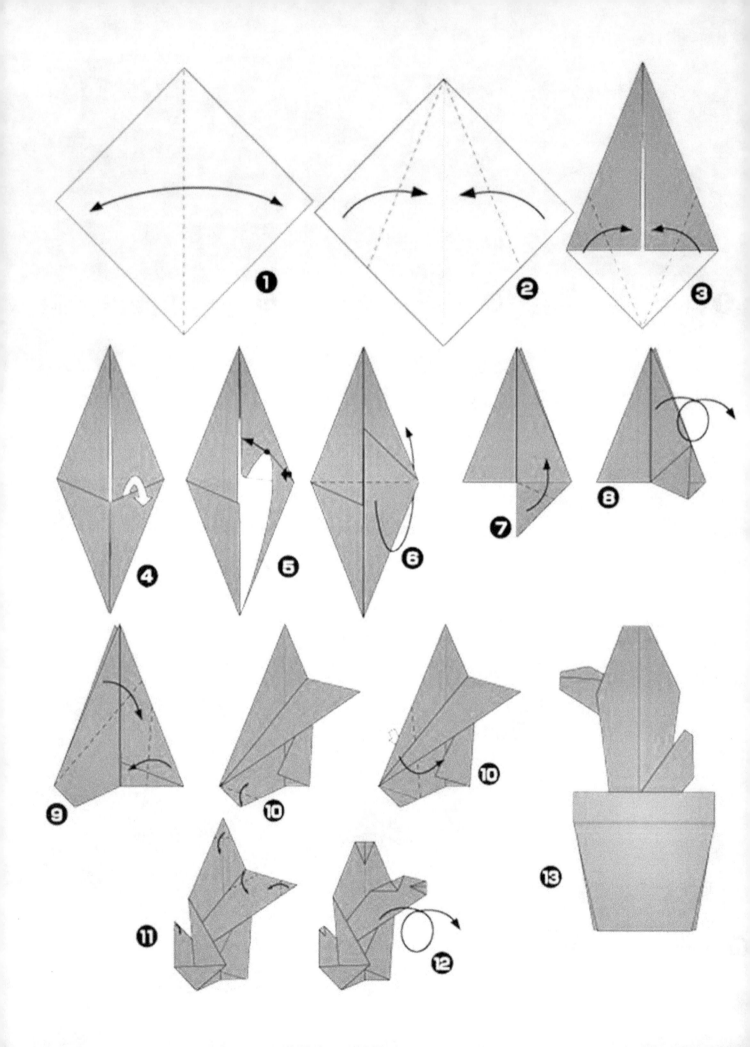

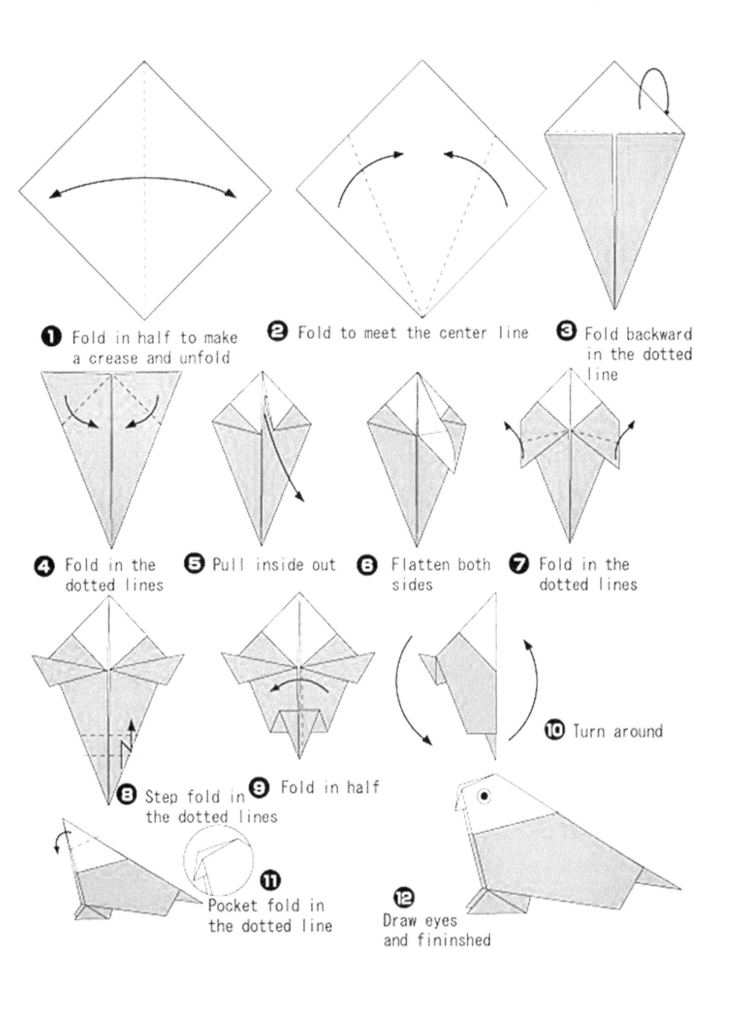

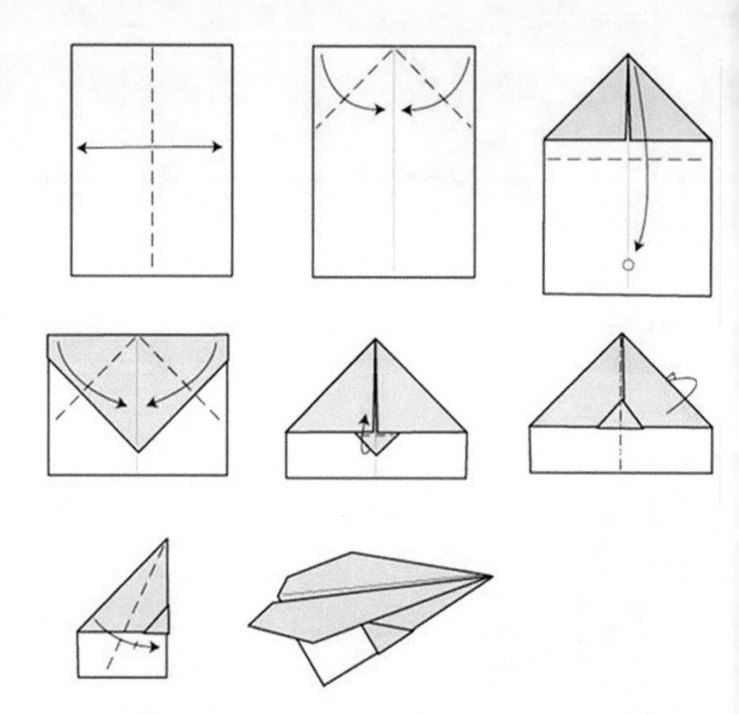

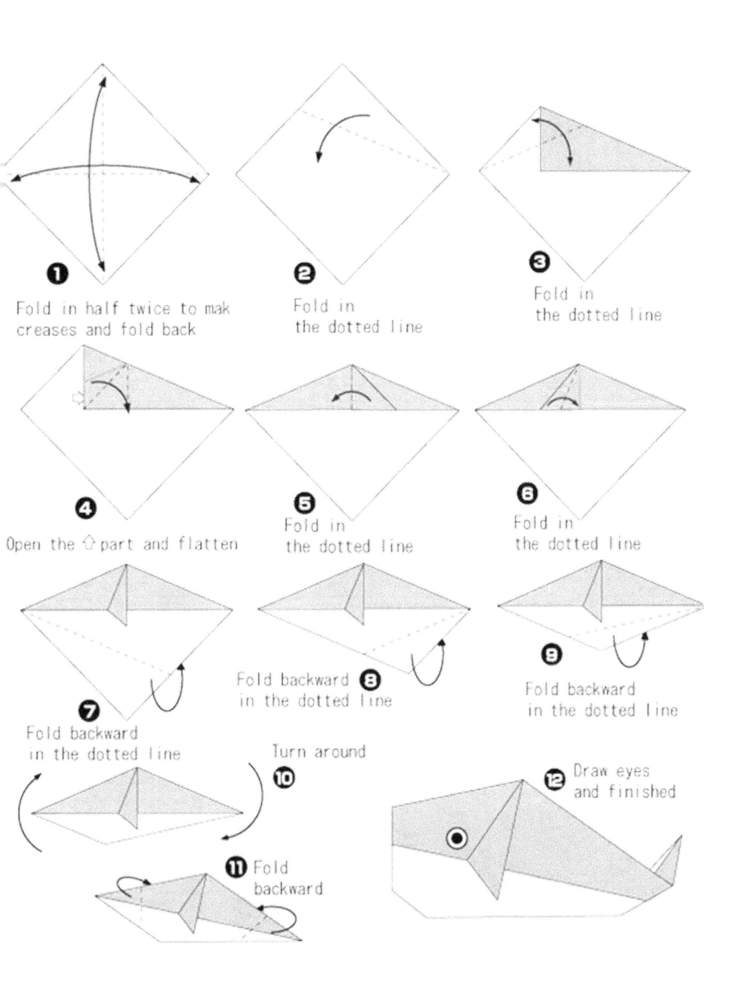

ANGELFISH

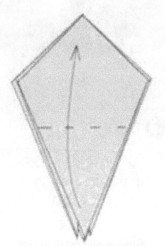

1. Begin with the bird base.

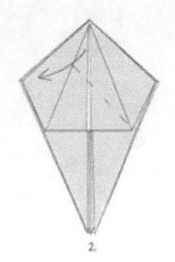

2.

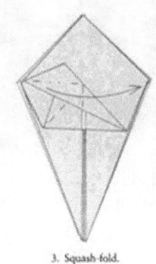

3. Squash-fold.

4.

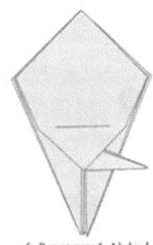

5. Repeat steps 1–4 behind.

6. Repeat behind.

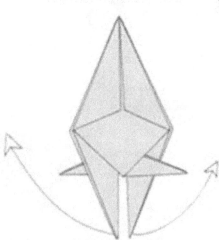

7. Pull out carefully.

8. ANGELFISH

www.ingramcontent.com/pod-product-compliance
Lightning Source LLC
Chambersburg PA
CBHW081046190125
20597CB00045B/1426